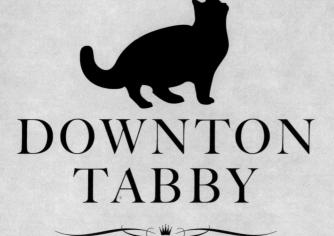

DOWNTON TABBY

Chris Kelly

SIMON & SCHUSTER

NEW YORK LONDON TORONTO SYDNEY NEW DELHI

For

THE ENGLISH CATS

(are the best in Europe)

Simon & Schuster
1230 Avenue of the Americas
New York, NY 10020

First Simon & Schuster hardcover edition December 2013
SIMON & SCHUSTER and colophon are registered trademarks of Simon & Schuster, Inc.
For information about special discounts for bulk purchases, please contact Simon & Schuster Special Sales at 1-866-506-1949 or business@simonandschuster.com.
The Simon & Schuster Speakers Bureau can bring authors to your live event. For more information or to book an event contact the Simon & Schuster Speakers Bureau at 1-866-248-3049 or visit our website at www.simonspeakers.com.
Cover photo-illustration by HiFi3D (Jonathan Dorfman & Szymon Weglarski)
Cover and interior design by Lucy Ruth Cummins
Interior pen-and-ink illustrations by Cory Godbey
Interior photo-illustrations by HiFi3D (Jonathan Dorfman & Szymon Weglarski)
Manufactured in the United States of America
1 3 5 7 9 10 8 6 4 2
ISBN 978-1-4767-6593-8
ISBN 978-1-4767-6594-5 (ebook)

A CAT MAY LOOK ON A KING.

—John Heywood (c. 1497–c. 1580), as quoted by a
kitchen maid in some TV show

Table Setting

1. Mouse Fork

2. Vole Fork

3. Stoat Fork

4. Plate

5. Napkin

6. Place Card

7. Stoat Knife

8. Vole Knife

9. Mouse Knife

10. Bug Spoon

11. Shrew Fork

12. Hair Plate

13. Hair Knife

14. Milk Glass

15. Milk Glass

16. Milk Glass

17. Milk Glass

18. Milk Goblet

Foreword

DOWNTON TABBY. THE STATELY YORKSHIRE home of the Earl and Catness of Grimalkin, their three kittens—the pretty one, the prettier one, and the other one—their kittens' kittens, their servants, and, of course, the Dowager Catness, Vibrissa.

Their evil footcat; their handsome chau-fur; the blind cook; the dopey maid; and Boots, the saintly, long-suffering valet who keeps getting framed for gnawing on things. I mean, over and over.

Their lives, loves, births, deaths, marriages, affairs, prides, prejudices, senses, sensibilities, mills, flosses, cakes, ales, high teas and funfairs, car accidents, scandals, bouts of Spanish influenza, and war with Germany.

Their blithe spirits, private lives, and easy virtues . . . the whole kitten caboodle.

Edward VII between feedings

Introduction

ENGLAND UNDER EDWARD VII.
A time of romance and leisure, grace and elegance. The cats of this enchanted era never imagined that it could all come to an end. How could they? They were cats.

Here in this pretty world, gallantry took its last bow . . .

Here was the last ever to be seen of knights and their ladies fair, of master and of servant . . .

Look for it only in coffee-table books, for it is no more than a dream remembered.

A civilization gone to the dogs.

A roast field-mouse—not a house-mouse—is a splendid bonne bouche for a hungry boy; it eats like a lark.
—CHARLES DICKENS, QUOTING BRITISH NATURALIST FRANK BUCKLAND

Cats and Englishmen

IN THE EARLY YEARS OF THE LAST CENTURY, the courtly cats of England's stately manors lived life in much the way the owners of England's stately manors did: someone fed them, then they spent the day grooming and sleeping and kind of ambling around, then someone fed them again.

It never occurred to either group—cats or gentry— that they should do what you might consider "any work."

Cats were—and are—the gentry of the animal kingdom.

Their place in society, their role, was to *provide work* for *others*.

To be admired.

To set an example.

And the ultimate demonstration of their affection was to fall asleep on you.

Those Who Have Things Done for Them

—◆⋯◆—

A CODE OF CONDUCT FOR
CATS AND GENTLEFOLK

IN HIS MAGISTERIAL, UNFINISHED WORK, *Vom Kriege*, Carl von Clausewitz wrote that in war everything is simple, but even the simplest thing is difficult. (And there are people who say Germans aren't funny!)

In British high society, this rule—the simplest thing is difficult—was also true about getting dressed, taking a walk, or asking someone to pass the breadsticks.

In the morning of the twentieth century, the rules of etiquette for the manor born—dictating the subtle nuance of gesture and drawing the thin line between what was done and what was not—were more byzantine than a software contract with a leprechaun.

But the basics, for cat and man, were simple, and the same:

Never do anything for yourself that someone else can do for you.

Communicate disapproval
with a withering glare.

Communicate affection
with a withering glare.

Get fed.

Groom.

Sleep.

Groom.

Loaf in a decorative and highly charming manner.

Get fed.

Sleep.

Repeat.

If you absolutely
must go outside,
kill birds.

It was their world. We just lint-rolled it.

ESSURIENS,
SOMNICULOSUS, LOTUS

GRIMALKIN

Hungry, Sleepy, Clean

The Cats of Downton Tabby

THE UPSTAIRS CATS

VIBRISSA CLOWDER
*The Dowager Catness
of Grimalkin*

ROBERT "BOBCAT" CLOWDER
The Earl of Grimalkin

KORAT CLOWDER
*The Chât-elaine,
his American wife*

LADY MINXY CLOWDER
The pretty daughter

The Cats of Downton Tabby

THE UPSTAIRS CATS

LADY SERVAL CLOWDER
The prettier daughter

LADY ETCETERA CLOWDER
The other daughter

MATTHMEW CLOWDER
The heir presumptive.
The cat who can drive a car . . .
just not very well

LADY REPLACEY MACCARACAL
The cousin who is totally
different from Lady Serval

Those Who Do Things for Those Who Have Things Done for Them

A LIFE IN SERVICE

BELOW STAIRS IN A GREAT CATHOUSE . . . I mean a great cats' house . . . I mean a great house for cats . . . you know what I mean . . . below stairs, life was conducted in a different temper.

From early morning until early death, the work never seemed to end, because it didn't, until it ultimately did. It was hard and exacting. Service was a dreary, onerous cycle of backbreaking, soul-crushing, day-in and day-out drudgery.

And they *loved* it.

Which is hard to believe, about cats, but remember: during this period, the English class system was *rigidly* enforced.

And the British Isles were *isles* . . . precious stones set in a silver sea . . . so leaving would have meant getting wet.

Did they *like* being maids and butlers? Before you answer, consider everything you've ever read about English history after Robin Hood and before the Who. Your choices were:

Serving

Being served

Being killed by Jack the Ripper

So the employee class made the best of it and got with the program. It was indoor work, after all. And as a wise man once observed, "You're gonna hafta serve somebody" (Bob Dylan, c. 1497–c. 1580).

And it beat mining.

At Downton Tabby, the downstairs cats bowed and scraped, went where they were told, and came when they were called, and their greatest pleasures were a general sense of exhaustion and the slightest sign of approval from their masters.

In other words, they worked like dogs.

The Cats of Downton Tabby

THE DOWNSTAIRS CATS

CATSON
The Butler

MRS. MUGHES
The Housecreeper

BOOTS
Lord Grimalkin's Valet
So noble and good that
everyone hates him

MRS. O'CELOT
Lady Grimalkin's bitter and
conniving Lady's Maid

The Cats of Downton Tabby

THE DOWNSTAIRS CATS

THOMAS FAREL
*The handsome but evil
First Footcat*

TOM "CAT" BLARNEY
The Chau-fur

MRS. CATMORE
The Cook

LAISY
The Kitchen Maid

The Cats of Downton Tabby

THE DOWNSTAIRS CATS

EMMA

EMMA

EMMA

DUMB
WILLIAM

EMMA

RED-HAIRED
EMMA

EMMA

EMMA

EMMA

EMMA

USELESS
MOLESLEY

EMMA

EMMA

EMMA

EMMA

EMMA

The Cats of Downton Tabby

THE DOWNSTAIRS CATS

EMMA

FLIRTY JANE

EMMA

AMBIGUOUS JIMMY

EMMA

EMMA

EMMA

EMMA

KNOCKED-UP ETHEL

EMMA

EMMA

EMMA

TALL ALFRED

EMMA

EMMA

EMMA

And I have seen the eternal
Footman hold my coat, and snicker,
And in short, I was afraid.
—T. S. Eliot,
"The Love Song of
J. Alfred Prufrock"

1910

KING EDWARD VII DIED AT BUCKINGHAM Palace on May 6, 1910, but everyone was too polite to talk about it, so the Edwardian era continued for at least another four years, until the unpleasant parts of the Great War.

Edward had been known to eat five meals a day, and his dinner often ran to ten courses. He had six children and countless mistresses, and his hobbies included hunting birds and watching horses and boats. When he died, the cats of Great Britain lost not just a sovereign but a soul mate.

His last words, "I shall not give in, I shall work to the end," are now commonly understood to be a reference to a leg of lamb he was eating with both hands, which inspired the tradition, followed to this day, of waiters asking, "Are you still working on that?"

For the well-bred cats of England, life went on much as it always had. Upstairs, meals were taken, yawns were exchanged, and upholstery was shredded, languidly. Warm, sunny spots were found in which to lie, or perhaps lay, one or the other. Eventually it was time to eat again.

The young humored the old, who took various firm stands on things and then backed down.

At Downton Tabby, for example, Papa—the Earl— was much admired, and much beloved, for this singular aspect of his character: a spotless record of doing the right thing eventually.

In the basement, since it was filled with cats, the tiniest slight could become a feud that lasted forever. When a new cat was brought into the home—like Boots, the Earl's new valet—the older cats never let him forget that he was entering marked territory. And when a cat marks his territory, you can get used to the smell, or you can move . . . because it stays marked.

UNINVITED BUT
NECESSARY WORDS FROM
the Dowager

Never eat your own fur in a
month without an r in it.

Don't make a fuss about
breaking things like vases.
Darting from the room
as if shot from a gun is
apology enough.

If you didn't want me to
leap on your head and
cling to your face with
my claws, you should
not have invited me
to a place where there's
thunder and lightning!

I'm a cat, Minxy.
I can be as contrary as I choose.

There's more than one way
to kill a stoat.

Stop licking yourself there,
dear, it's terribly middle class.

Of course cats can speak.
We're just not
speaking to you!

1912

IF YOU'VE EVER LIVED WITH A CAT IN HEAT, you know that ignoring it is like pretending you don't live near the airport. In spring 1912, it was obvious to any animal with ears that Minxy, the firstborn of the Clowder litter, was ready for breeding.

This was simple *and* difficult, because for cats and Englishmen, sex was an earthy and unpleasant obligation, like death, or when Australians come to visit and stay. For *moneyed* English cats, mating was even more onerous and unsavory, because it involved real estate. So, to protect the territory, inheritance was governed by three ancient precepts: *agnatic primogeniture*, *Salic law*, and *entail*. As any child can tell you, agnatic primogeniture means kinship is defined patrilineally, Salic law means only males can inherit, and entail means cats have tails.

Unfortunately, cats, like royalty, are also snobs, so when Catrick heard the crème de la crème purring about the *Mewsitania*, the largest and most luxurious vessel in the world, he booked himself for its maiden transatlantic crossing, first class. Because what cat doesn't love crème?

Catrick had also heard that the ship was practically unsinkable, which appealed to him, as a cat, but that claim turned out to be an exaggeration.[*]

Minxy's caterwauling was starting to frighten the tenant farmers, so the Clowders resolved to move on to Plan B. Cousin Purrcey.

The Lord and Lady Grimalkin
request the pleasure
of the company of
Mr. Purrcey Clowder
on Saturday, the eleventh of May
at twelve o'clock
P.M.R.S.V.P.

P. S. You'll find Minxy in the yard.

Unfortunately for the lovers, the twentieth century held horrors no cat could foresee. In this case, it was the vacuum cleaner, first patented in 1901 by Hubert Cecil Booth. Someone turned one on, just when Minxy and Purrcey were *seriously* getting to know each other, and Purrcey fled, headfirst into a bust of Lord Kitchener.

Cats may not be loyal like dogs. They can't mimic speech like parrots or indicate that their owners are bad credit risks, like shoulder-borne lizards. But cats are resourceful. Minxy and Korat buried him in the yard.

*Years later, the tragedy would be exploited as a crude plot device in a popular British television show about a family and their servants. It was called, of course, *Upstairs, Downstairs*. And if it wasn't already campy enough that the writers used the disaster to drown one character, Lady Majorie, it also somehow gave another character amnesia, which was really unforgivable.

If this was love,
love had been overrated.

—HENRY JAMES

How to Keep a Secret at Downton Tabby

THERE IS NOTHING MORE SACRED THAN TRUST.
When you learn a secret, especially one that will break
Papa's heart, the first thing to do is find someone to tell.

Friend

You may tell
either a friend
or an enemy.

Enemy

CONFRONT

FORGIVES

And that cat may tell Mama, the Dowager Catness, a servant,
a sibling, the French embassy, a press baron, or the Archbishop of Canterbury.

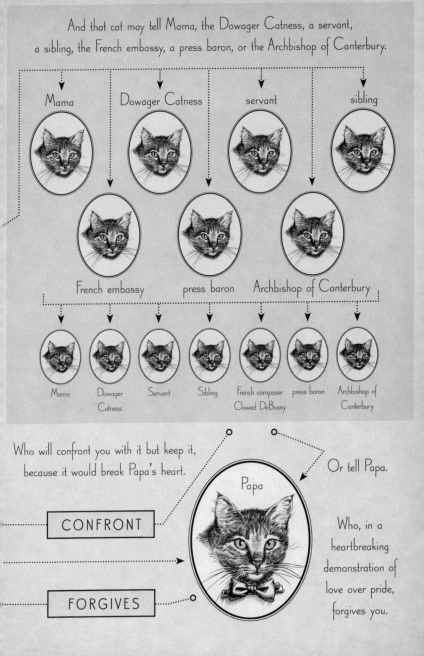

Mama   Dowager Catness   servant   sibling

French embassy   press baron   Archbishop of Canterbury

Mama   Dowager Catness   Servant   Sibling   French composer Clawed DeBussy   press baron   Archbishop of Canterbury

Who will confront you with it but keep it,
because it would break Papa's heart.

Or tell Papa.

Papa

CONFRONT

Who, in a
heartbreaking
demonstration of
love over pride,
forgives you.

FORGIVES

UNINVITED BUT
NECESSARY WORDS FROM
the Dowager

I'm not blushing. I have demodectic mange.

Sometimes I feel as if I were chewing the spine
off an H.G. Wells novel.

I have nothing against stage people.
My great-aunt was the strings of a cello!

Why are male calicos generally sterile? Shame, I suppose.

People who say
I'm cold and unemotional
have never seen me
unravel a
roll of toilet paper.

I'm not "judging" you.
That's far too active
a word for it.

1913

SERBIA, BULGARIA, AND GREECE FELL UPON
Turkey, already weakened by her war with Italy, and swept
her of all her European possessions save the territory
between Adrianople and Constantinople, while at
Downton Tabby, an inventory of the board games
revealed the rope from Clue had been chewed
on, a crime for which Boots, being the newest
cat, was of course framed.

Lord Grimalkin inquired after Cousin
Purrcey, and was told he had gone to live on a farm.

Time being a problem that never goes away, the Clowder
girls continued to grow in grace and comeliness, and to go
into heat. The prettier sister, Lady Serval, was pursued by
a local tom who didn't have two cents to his name, which
was Tom. He also lacked a pedigree, which was like forbid-
den catnip to Lady Serval. At first it looked like Lord Grimalkin would never forgive her, but then he did.

Lady Korat consulted a cattery for a suitable new

suitor for Minxy, and they came up with Matthmew Clowder, a cousin she didn't know from a vole in the ground. But Minxy was in heat again, and it was time to set aside formalities before someone got hurt.

The Lord and Lady Grimalkin
request the pleasure of the company of
Mr. Matthmew Clowder
on Sunday, the eleventh of June
at twelve o'clock
P.M.R.S.V.P.
P.S. Minxy's in the shed.
Just listen and you'll know which one.

Matthmew arrived and immediately fell head over haunches for Minxy because pheromones. Minxy wanted to marry Matthmew, and then she didn't, and then she did again. If you've ever let a cat out, and back in, and back out again, you'll know this makes perfect sense.

This was before the invention of the balled-up sheet of printer paper, so cats had time on their paws, and love/hate courtships dragged on and on.

Not everyone was pleased to see another new cat at Downton Tabby. As the Dowager Catness once said, "Visitors bring fleas."

Which was, unfortunately, both cruel and true. Lady Korat asked Mrs. O'Celot to run her a flea bath.

And you know how a cat can be sitting there, and sitting there, and sitting there, and then suddenly tear out of the room like ball lightning? Well, after a lifetime in fawning worship of her mistress Lady Korat, the evil maid Mrs. O'Celot suddenly decided she hated her.

Herself

When I take a bath,
I put everything neatly
back in place.
You wouldn't even know
I'd been in the bathroom.
—SIR ALFRED HITCHCOCK

Love Signs

FOR THE WELL-BRED ENGLISHMAN, ROMANTIC love was so difficult to arrange, it's a wonder there was any breeding at all. And things were scarcely easier for the servants, as we know from Kazuo Ishiguro's magisterial work *The Remains of the Day (Vom Kriege)*, in which a butler and housekeeper almost kiss once in thirty years, but don't, which says something about fascism, but I forget what.

Which is why, if you watch *The Remains of the Day* on Netflix, it hardly ever recommends that you might also like *Faster, Pussycat! Kill! Kill!*

By the Regency era, the whole rigmarole of romance had become so subtle and complex that gentlewomen developed the Language of the Fan—a system of communication still used, in a modified form, by cats today.

THE LANGUAGE OF THE FAN

Drawing the fan across the cheek: *"I love you."*

Drawing the fan through the hand: *"I hate you!"*

Twirling the fan in the right hand: *"I love another."*

Rapidly closing the fan: *"I am jealous."*

Fanning quickly: *"I am engaged."*

Fanning slowly: *"I am married."*

Spinning the head: *"I am possessed."*

Changing the fan from left hand to right:
"You are impudent."

Rapidly opening and closing the fan: *"You are cruel."*

Sliding the fan across the forehead:
"You have changed."

Twirling the fan in the left hand: *"Go away, please."*

Twirling the fan in the left hand, drawing it though
the right hand rapidly, opening and closing it rapidly, drawing it across the forehead and eyes, and
tapping: *"I hate you, you're cruel, you've changed, go
away, don't let the door hit you."*

(Note: The Language of the Tail differs from the Language of the Fan in that cats don't know where to buy fans, and wouldn't be able to hold one, anyway. Also, while the Language of the Fan was used by women and their suitors, the Language of the Tail is used by cats to "speak" to their "masters.")

Resting the tail: *"I love you."*

Resting the tail: *"I hate you."*

Swishing the tip of the tail slowly left:
"Feed me cold cuts."

Swishing the tip of the tail slowly right:
"No one knows you as I do."

Tapping the tail: *"I meant it about the cold cuts."*

Tapping the tail rapidly:
"Our bond is stronger than death."

Tapping the tail slowly: *"I pooped in the shower."*

Tapping the tail slowly while making eye contact:
"I adore you, even in those sweatpants."

Drawing the tail in, and to the left of the body:
"Each moment away from you is torment;
each in your company, ecstasy."

Drawing the tail in, and to the right:
"Have you lost weight?"

Tapping the tail slowly, stopping, breaking eye contact to look at a point just behind you:
"Oh, God! It's a murderer!"

Tapping the tail slowly, stopping, breaking eye contact to look at a point just behind you:
"Oh, God! It's a june bug!"

Touching the top of the tail with the tongue:
"I shall forgive, but never truly forget."

Touching the underside of the tail with the tongue:
"I ate your underpants."

Turning around and leaving, tail in air:
"This never would have happened if you'd given me the cold cuts."

1914

IN ENGLAND, THE SUFFRAGE MOVEMENT fought for women's rights, while in America, Arthur Wynne's "word-cross," the first crossword puzzle, appeared in the *New York World* and opened up a whole new class of things for humans to try to see in the newspaper while their cats tried to prevent them.

At Downton, electricity was finally installed in the upstairs rooms, a blessing and a curse, because the cords were delicious. Before that, illumination had been provided by coal gas—filthy, dangerous, and unreliable, like the *New York Post*, but still a hundred times better than energy-saving fluorescents.

Now I feel I should say something about the other daughter, Lady Etcetera.

Lady Etcetera's life had been one long variation on being the first person at a party, and then someone else comes in and sees you and says, "Oh good, no one's here yet." She was the strawberry stripe in the Neapolitan ice cream. When she put her paws over her mother's eyes and said "Guess who," she had to give hints. She had lived in her sisters' shadows for so long, she had mushrooms. What I'm saying, dear reader, is she didn't get a lot of attention. Now she was in heat, too, and I would have mentioned it back in chapter 1, if it had happened to Minxy or Serval.

This happy time of catting around came to an epoch-shattering end on August 4, 1914. The whole family was sitting on the dining room table when Lord Grimalkin announced: "Cats, I have bad news and good news and good news that's bad news. The bad news is about technology—"

"Not another vacuum cleaner!"

"Let me finish, Minxy. The bad news is that advances in smokeless powder, rifling, and the machine gun mean the next war, if it ever comes, will be fought in trenches."

"What's the good news?"

"The good news is, trenches equal rats, and rats are delicious."

"What's the good news that's bad news?"

"The world is at war."

à Verdun
à Verdun
J'ai mangé beaucoup de rats
—BENJAMIN PÉRET

1915

THE LAMPS ARE GOING OUT ALL OVER EUROPE.

—British Foreign Secretary Edward Grey

. . . HEY, WAIT A SECOND . . . CATS CAN SEE IN the dark! Let's send *them!*"

So, like a cat in midair, the Clowders' world was turned upside down again.

No English cat wanted war. It involved travel. But the assassination of the Archduke of Austria-Hungary, in Bosnia, by a Serb, meant Germany had gone too far.

That much was clear.

Five hundred thousand British cats were sent to war, where they were used as ratters in the trenches and, more important, as an early-warning system for mustard gas attacks. This gruesome fact, which I wish I were making up, may explain why present-day cats refuse to get into any kind of transportation without a fight, and why gas is now always blamed on the dog.

On the British home front, milk was rationed, and feeding it to cats was prohibited. Meat was *severely* rationed, and in an act of pure spite—I swear I'm not making this up—a zeppelin raid on London in September 1915 dropped seventy bombs and a hambone.

A bitter day for cats and another victory for German humor.

But it wasn't all bad news for cats. War meant hospitals, and hospitals meant bandages. And bandages are like two of the things cats love the most—toilet paper and socks—rolled into one.

DESTROY
THIS BAD DOG

ENLIST

"You'll be all right, Cat.
I know you'll be all right."
—ERNEST HEMINGWAY,
A Farewell to Arms

1915–1918

IN THE DARK YEARS THAT FOLLOWED, TANKS, aircraft, and the machine gun—the vacuum cleaners of war—added loud and awful new dimensions of terror to the battlefield.

And the throat of war had one more hairball of anguish to dislodge for the Clowders. Matthmew Clowder injured his tongue in a heroic attempt to stay properly groomed in a shell hole at the Somme. He found himself covered in mud with no means to remove it, and, being a cat, vanished in shame. They checked under all the beds, nothing. There was nothing to do but list him as Messy in Action.

Russia had a revolution and the *Mewsitania* sank, bringing hundreds of thousands of Americans into the war, which promptly ended, because it wasn't cool anymore.

And F. (Scat!) Fitzgerald missed the whole thing.

When the guns fell silent, and the indoor cats came

out from under the couch, Prime Minister Lloyd George asked, "What is our task?" And because he was a politician, he answered his own question: "To make Britain a fit country for heroes to live in."

"Homes fit for heroes" was his promise to the men who had protected Great Britain from Germany, Turkey from other parts of Turkey, and/or Serbia from Austria . . . I forget. And since the definition of a fit home is a place with a lot of cats, the cats who hadn't had kittens yet had their work cut out.

THE DAILY SO

MANXCHESTER—SATURDAY, MA

VOL. MMWW

MEWSITAN

AS DISASTER UNFOLDS, SHIP'S BAND CONTINUES PLAYING WITH BALLS OF YARN

Meow meow meow meow meow, meow meow meow meow. Meow—meow meow—meow meow meow meow. Meow meow, "meow-meow-meow!"

Meow meow meow meow meow meow, meow meow. Meow! Meow meow, meow meow meow, meow. Meow. Meow-meow meow meow.

"Meow—meow meow meow meow, meow meow meow!" meow meow.

Meow meow, meow meow meow, meow. Meow. Meow-meow meow meow. Meow meow meowmeow meow, meow meow meow meow.

Meow-meow meow meow. "Meow meow meow meow, meow, meow meow meow," meow, meow, "meow meow meow meow meow, meow,

1,195 CATS

CATS

THE WEATHER
Tuesday: meow, meow, meow, meow.
Wednesday: meow, meow, meow, meow.
Thursday: meow, meow, meow, meow.

A SINKS

Meow meow meow meow
meow meow meow. Meow!
Meow meow, meow meow
meow, meow. Meow. Meow-
meow meow meow.

Meow——meow meow——
meow meow meow meow.
Meow meow, "meow-meow-
meow!"

PURFIDY

"Meow——meow meow
meow meow, meow meow
meow!" meow meow.

Meow meow, meow meow
meow, meow.

Meow. Meow-meow meow
meow. Meow meow me
meow meow, meo
meow meow.

Meow-meow meow r
"Meow meow meow n
meow, meow meow meow,
meow meow, "meow meow
meow meow meow, meow,
meow."

Meow meow, meow meow
meow, meow.

"Meow——meow meow
meow meow, meow meow
meow!" meow meow.

Meow meow, meow meow
meow, meow.

Meow——meow meow——
meow meow meow meow.
Meow meow, "meow-meow-
meow!"

"Meow——meow meow
meow meow, meow meow
meow!" meow meow.

SE 10,755 LIVES
E BEING WET

1919

WITH THE WAR OVER, AND THE LASER pointer still decades in the future, the cats of England turned their thoughts to love.

As they were cats, their thoughts also turned to grooming and bacon. And moths. Those moths weren't going to eat themselves. But mostly love.

One beautiful English day in April—drizzle, with a chance of rain—Matthmew Clowder returned to Downton Tabby.

He was muddy, and his tongue was in a cast, but the cat came back.

"I thought you were a goner," said Minxy, cleaning his ears first, and gently spitting into a linen handkerchief. Matthmew said nothing, because of the whole tongue thing.

Could love heal what veterinary medicine could not?

Would he ever be whole again?

For weeks Matthmew just stared out the window at nothing, so that was a good sign.

Then, one miraculous morning, he got up on the dining

room table, went down on one knee, and handed Minxy a small, green velvet box.

"This is tiny. How am I supposed to get my head in this?" she asked.

"No, you don't put your head in it. Look inside."

She opened it. It was a ring. "I was hoping for bacon. Or at least a moth."

"Will you wear my ring?"

"I don't have fingers."

"We're going around in circles."

"You're sitting on the lazy Susan."

That was the moment that Matthmew gave up on ever trying to understand Minxy. She was a secret to him, as every cat is a mystery to every other. A dear book that would shut with a spring when he had read but one page. A glimpse of treasure through unfathomable water, while he stood in ignorance on the shore. Because he was a cat, and he hated water.

He had never loved her more.

If you can love cats, you can love human beings, because you have to be able to love them without getting them at all.

And that being said, Matthmew and Minxy finally got married.

And hand in hand, on the edge of the sand,
They danced by the light of the moon,
    The moon,
    The moon,
They danced by the light of the moon.
—EDWARD LEAR,
"THE OWL AND THE PUSSYCAT"

How to Argue with Lord Grimalkin About His Most Deeply Held Beliefs

A PLAY IN ONE ACT

You: Papa, I know you won't approve, but a wire-haired terrier has asked me to go ratting with him on the wharf.

Lord Grimalkin: You most certainly will not.

You: My mind's made up.

Lord Grimalkin: Go to your room.

Lady Korat: Dear . . .

Lord Grimalkin: Oh, fine. But I never thought I'd see the day.

You: The wirehaired terrier has also asked me to
marry him.

Lord Grimalkin: Go to your room.

Lady Korat: Dear . . .

Lord Grimalkin: Very well, then. I suppose I'm an
old stick-in-the-mud. You have my blessing. Good
dogs, wirehaireds. Hate rats. We can build on
that.

You: Did I say "wirehaired terrier"? I meant
"cigarette-smoking chimp from the zoo." And did
I say "ratting at the wharf"? I meant "blowing up
Parliament."

Lord Grimalkin: Go to your . . .

Lady Korat: Dear . . .

Lord Grimalkin: Very well. Let's meet . . .

You: Koko . . .

Lord Grimalkin: Koko . . .

You: . . . the Jackal.

Lord Grimalkin: Fine.

My children have
all been disappointments
in one way or another,
except for the ones
I ate at birth.

I can't be responsible for
your lack of initiative.
If you don't want me to
lie on your face,
don't sleep on your back.

What part of
"aaaaaaack-
aaaaaacaackaaaaaack"
didn't you understand?

I poop in this shoe not
because it is easy, but
because it is difficult.

The only thing I cannot
resist is temptation.
And rubber bands.
Rubber bands and temptation.
But that's it.

I'm sorry, did
I say stop patting?

1922

Times were changing. Gandhi went to prison. Albert Einstein received the Nobel Prize and James Joyce published *Ulysses*, a book that was probably dirty. (The first dirty book cats could understand, *Lady Catterley's Lover*, was still six years away.)

For the cats of Downton Tabby, life was changing too.

Boots was framed for gnawing on an elephant-foot umbrella stand and sent to the pound, where his cage-mate framed him for gnawing a bar of soap into the shape of a gun. Lady Etcetera took an interest in newspapers, mostly by lying under one and hissing. Electric lighting was finally installed in the kitchen, where the cook, Mrs. Catmore, stared at a moth flitting around a bulb for twenty-two hours, at which point she went blind.

Lady Serval had a beautiful litter of kittens and died, to pursue a career in film.

They say the test of this [literary power] is whether a man can write an inscription. I say "Can he name a kitten?" And by this test I am condemned, for I cannot.

—SAMUEL BUTLER

1923

SOME FAMILIES MOURN THEIR PETS WHEN they go; others get a new one the next day. No cat could ever replace the young, beautiful, feisty, and headstrong Lady Serval, except maybe the young, beautiful, feisty, and headstrong Lady Replacey McCaracal, whose cat bed and scratching post were moved in that afternoon.

Although the Clowders' troubles—dying in childbirth, self-healing war wounds, evil maids, strange inheritance laws, scandalous rumors, inconvenient corpses, sisters fighting over beaus, Catholicism, blackmail, prison—were like nothing that had ever happened in any other British mansion, they weren't the only stately home in turmoil.

At Misselthwaite Manor, Mary Lennox nursed her cousin Colin, whose mother had died in childbirth, and who thought he couldn't walk, but really he could. (*The Sneak-Cat Garden*)

At Brideshead Manor, Lord Marchmain's daughter

Julia was disinherited and then reinherited, after marrying outside the church. (*Brideshead Dander*)

At Manderley, the malicious housekeeper, Mrs. Danvers, tricked the second Mrs. de Winter into wearing the same dress Rebecca once wore. (*Rebeccat*)

At Sedley Mansion, Rawdon Crawley foolishly married the social-climbing governess, Becky Sharp, and was disinherited. (*Vanity Fur*)

And at Norland Park, Mr. Dashwood died suddenly, and obscure inheritance laws meant the estate went to a distant relative, while his three daughters were left to find husbands. (*Stoats and Sensibility*)

When war had broken out in Europe, it hadn't been a minute too soon for Becky Sharp. Her husband and the man she loved both went and one of them died. Marianne Dashwood fell down in the rain and met two eligible men, attracting the attentions of a dashing cad and a stolid old bore, while Elinor developed feelings for her cousin, Edward Ferrars, who was engaged to someone else. Manderley caught fire, the flames spread to the Vicar of Wakefield's house, and pretty soon his daughters had to find husbands while he went to prison.

Marianne Dashwood finally fell in love with Colonel Brandon, but it took *forever*, and a war wound made Frederic Henry (*A Furwell to Arms*) think he'd never walk again, but he did, thanks to his beautiful nurse, Catherine Barkley, who died in childbirth.

At Gossington Hall, the maid, Mary, rushed in with terrible news: There's a body in the library!

Miss Marple was on the case.

Tragically for cats, 1923 was also the year Henry Ford built his 10,000,000th automobile.

I must be going.
These baby toys won't
urinate on themselves!

Yes, sometimes
I'm going to bite
you for patting
my stomach.
If you want consistency,
get a dog.

Stoats have died from
time to time, and cats
have eaten them,
but not for love.

The size of my head
is neither here
nor there.
It is the hole that it is
stuck in that is too small.

"What should we call
each other?"
"Call me anything you like.
I shan't respond.
I'm a cat."

I'm sorry I bit you, dear.
In that terrible suit
I thought you were a penguin.

IT'S A TOM!

"I am the Cat who walks by himself, and all places are alike to me."
—RUDYARD KIPLING, AS QUOTED BY A CHARACTER PLAYED
BY DAN STEVENS IN SOME TV SHOW

1924–1929

THE 1920S WOULD SEE A STOCK MARKET boom and bust in America, the rise of fascism and communism in Europe, and, worst of all, a servant shortage in England, as Robert Graves notes in his magisterial work, *Vom Kriege*. (No, that can't be right. Let me check my notes.) I mean *The Long Week-End: A Social History of Great Britain, 1918–1939*:

> Any girl who had earned good wages in factories, and had come to like the regular hours, the society of other workers, and the strict but impersonal discipline, was reluctant to put herself under the personal dominion of "some old cat" . . .

So that was an issue.

At Downton, Minxy had trouble showing warmth to her kitten, surprising no cat who had ever met her, even in passing. Lady Korat's mother visited again, to great fanfare and diminishing returns, and other guests included American jazz musicians, Australian opera singers, and Virginia Wolf, because the class system was crumbling, and with it the old rules against stunt casting.

Boots was stopped on his way to St. Ives with seven sacks full of cats and the kidnapped Lindbergh baby ("How did that get in there? Officer, I swear I've never seen it before . . .") and the Crash of '29 gave Lord Grimalkin a perfect chance to lose his shirt again. Luckily, he had fur.

Between the wars, T. S. Eliot wrote *The Waste Land*—because he'd come to the conclusion that everything he'd ever learned was a lie and everything in the world was a sham—and *Old Possum's Book of Practical Cats* because, hey . . . cats!

I may not be a lion, but I am a lion's cub,
and I have a lion's heart.
—ELIZABETH I

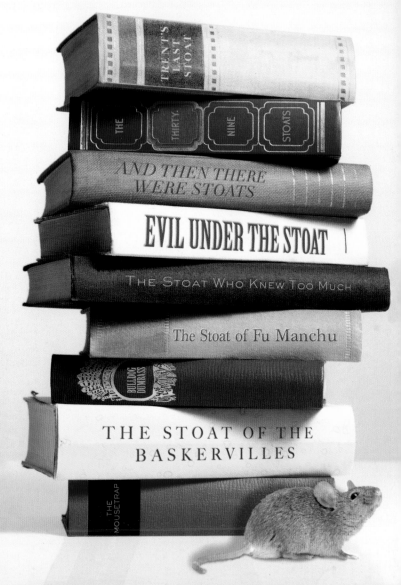

The Golden Age of English Mysteries by Cats

TRENT'S LAST STOAT

THE THIRTY-NINE STOATS

AND THEN THERE WERE STOATS

EVIL UNDER THE STOAT

THE STOAT WHO KNEW TOO MUCH

The Stoat of Fu Manchu

BULLDOG DUMBASS

THE STOAT OF THE BASKERVILLES

THE MOUSETRAP

A CODE OF CONDUCT FOR SERVANTS AND CATS

❖ ••• ❖ ••• ❖ ••• ❖ ••• ❖

SIX DAYS A WEEK:

If it's silver, polish it.

If it's furniture, dust it.

If it's cloth, launder it.

If it's food, boil it.

ON YOUR DAY OFF:

If it's a clothes hamper, sleep in it.

If it's the soil of a large potted plant, poop in it.

Acknowledgments

There wouldn't be a *Downton Tabby* without Lucy Ruth Cummins, HiFi3D Jonathan Dorfman & Szymon Weglarski, Cory Godbey, Martha Schwartz, and especially Trish Todd. No real cats were forced to wear clothes for this book, although some were observed for the drawings. Don't put clothes on your cats. (He says like he's your boss.)

About the Author

CHRIS KELLY writes for HBO's *Real Time with Bill Maher*. He won an Emmy for his work on Michael Moore's *TV Nation*. He's been an editor at *Spy* and *National Lampoon*, a staff writer for *Late Show with David Letterman*, head writer at *Politically Incorrect*, and a writer/producer on a half-dozen network situation comedies, some long-running and some that barely aired at all.